FORGET THE LAKE

for Aunt Teresa and Leah

FORGET THE LAKE

Mary Turley-McGrath

Mary Turley-McGrath

ARLEN
HOUSE

FORGET THE LAKE

is published in 2014 by
ARLEN HOUSE
42 Grange Abbey Road
Baldoyle
Dublin 13
Ireland
Phone: 00 353 86 8207617
Email: arlenhouse@gmail.com
arlenhouse.blogspot.com

International distribution
SYRACUSE UNIVERSITY PRESS
621 Skytop Road, Suite 110
Syracuse, NY 13244–5290
Phone: 315–443–5534/Facs: 315–443–5545
Email: supress@syr.edu
www.syracuseuniversitypress.syr.edu

978–1–85132–093–6, paperback

Design ¦ Arlen House

'Waterfall' by Frankie Gallagher
2005, oil on canvas
reproduced courtesy of the artist
galfrankie@gmail.com

CONTENTS

FORGET THE LAKE

WATERLINES

LAKE SONG

Sometimes I try to forget the lake,
to forget:
that mile-long stretch of water overhung by woods;
and the mid-rib of current by the boathouse where
every day the dance began when midday sun drank
cascading diamonds from the lake's caldera,
then spilled and spread swathes of silver fire.

Sometimes I try to forget the lake,
to forget:
afternoon calm as Jonah unlocked the boathouse door,
dropped clanking chains that tied the boat to iron rings.
Light danced on the oaken oars; the further out he rowed
across green-brown water, I knew it was his lake,
     not mine;
at last he swivelled in the oars, set them clattering on the
     floor,
gazed at sky and earth to see his share of Eden's Garden.

Sometimes I try to forget the lake,
to forget:
orange sunsets as Rachel carried her book into my room,
her book of the *Otherworld*; when she read, it made her
     cry;
it made me cry too, but I cried inside, showing her
     nothing.
Nothing can bring back the dead, the silent, the forgotten;
some have their names on the Wall, some wrongly
     written,
some with no names at all, their eyes gone forever.
When she read her book, the lake was grey as lead.

Sometimes I try to forget the lake,
to forget:

the full moon in July beyond tall shuttered windows,
taking her place in a cloudy sky above the withered
water.

I waited for her incline, saw her escape fettering clouds
until she reigned alone. A shaft of moonlight split
the room, reached the roses by my bed.

UNDERMUSIC

Sunday bells brought
late morning greyness
with long candles of light
squeezed between shutters.
Speckles of soot pecked
crumpled white pages
thrown in the grate.

Below the window,
from a pipe-trickle
by the sandstone steps,
water-lute music rose.
For an hour it played,
then faded with the mist

TRANSITIONS

The lake became an estuary overnight;
besieged by hammering rain,
flattened, subdued to shallows
of dark foil-strips between trees.
The drooping hazels and alders offered
no consolation; the sky was falling,
impaling itself on tips of forest pines;
it descended to enwrap the lake.

The heron had left for the lawn,
neck pushed forward in disdain;
the deluge had soaked him
to an alabaster shape. Then, near
the copper beech, he took flight
across the grass and was gone.

DUSK AT RATHMULLAN

A road moulded to the shape of the shore;
nothing between it and the rocks
but a low hedge of copper beech,
its leaves rolled up in the cold.

Above the strand the sky turned pewter,
released short bursts of rain;
evening sunlight funnelled
to make a spotlight tracing
the flight-path of gulls.

They fanned out and banked to the east,
absorbed shades of silver,
mercury and opal grey,
the sheen off gunmetal,
then vanished into light.

Where rocks jutted along the sands,
shells littered the tidemark;
the sea's treasure trove:
scallops and razor shells,
all open and empty;

near them lunulae of thin mother of pearl
in pink, green and blue,
transparent as skin melting
into air, to escape the break
of waves on infinite sands.

RATHLIN

The moon over Rathlin
scans the Sea of Moyle,
as it licks the rocks
below the road at the end
of the pebble-covered garden.

Moonlight selects the waves
in pulses of dark and light,
turns them to a phalanx of soldiers
carrying black spears, racing
to hide in the rocks.

When clouds heave away
towards the West Lighthouse,
the sky becomes the shimmering
abalone shell I gave you
when we stayed in your house

near the Black Castle. We slept
that night to the deep sea's moan,
so I felt I had been borrowed
by the sea, and returned home
with the morning sun.

CANAL

Winter sun triumphs over ghostly office blocks
near Baggot Street, spills on canal water, spins
a golden silk-road edged with maple leaves
worn brittle, like papyrus pages from books
of the Manicheans, the lost religion of light.

Along the asphalt path, roots split the surface
on their blind journey to curves and indents
trowelled out by the kiss of constant water,
transparent half-way to the other bank.

Linen-thread heads of bulrushes quiver, nudged
by the empty beer cans that glint garishly,
flashing out faux Morse signals:
the world is past itself, alive, revelling
in morning beauty, revived, renewed.

Water-hens flick up and down along the brink,
then dart back in; their hoots echo to one another
from beaks like lit matches against the gloss
of black plumage. Soon they are gone, hidden
in a mazed world of reeds, bulrushes, grass.

Two curved iron pipes are clamped to the side
of the bridge – there for a hundred years at least –
like dolphins in suspended animation, ready
to leap and play with the yellow bouncy ball
bobbing aimlessly at the arched stonework.

Beyond the bridge the water is still; then comes
the raucous calls of two mallards in mid-stream;
extended wings hurl cascades of droplets,
scintillating bodies vibrate in green and brown,
movement is lost in radiance.

RIVER OF THE WILLOWS

This river is my muse, my goddess,
roping through my senses night and day.

I watched from the bridge; March air stung my skin,
and not finding it cold enough to mingle with itself,

left me looking at black water, streaked with orange
    lights,
that sped onwards to the abbey walls.

Where land and water merge, knotted and stitched
    together
by the reeds, gifts of the goddess lay hidden:

pendants of jade, amber beads, bronze amulets,
our gifts to her long ago, before we left her banks

of wolves and boar, to build a crannóg on the lake.
Others came with us, those who feared the tribe:

the makers of images from wood and antler,
shamans and singers of poems and songs.

We filled the lake bed with boulders, dug gravel
from the shoreline; our axes split

the trees we floated out to make the centre posts
and palisade, our houses roofed with long dried reeds.

Burning was the end of it: the tribe's fire-arrows
floated from the sky; flames licked the outer timbers,
ran below the platform; the boats burned tied to their
posts.

My goddess knew; they were coming for her gifts;
she gave no sign.

BOATYARD

The main shed is a study in chaos;
two smaller side sheds are no better;

fumes from wood glue stab
my nose and head like needles.

So many boats at different stages
of growth or decay:

an old fishing boat frame
like the rib cage of a stranded whale;

the cruiser *Atlantis* on a platform,
poised on its funeral pyre.

More than enough here for a thousand
abstract paintings.

THE BLUE BOY

The sea had slipped out so far from the beach,
so far out, it seemed to belong somewhere else.

Weekend crowds swamped the loose sands:
parents with picnic baskets, grannies in floppy hats,
grandads with deck chairs, kids in summer clothes.

The boy in dark-blue shorts and t-shirt, flopped
    facedown
on the level sand, his fair curls reflecting the sun.
He dug fingers and toes into the grains, nailing
himself to them.
He roared – not just a roar, a cry-roar –
like a seal calf abandoned by his mother.

He had not been banished by the others;
his sister ran to him in her candy-pink swimsuit,
lifted him, but he bellowed all the more and
    dropped down again.

Did he want the sea to come back, did he think it had
    gone forever,
and he would never get the chance to swim or paddle?

At last, his father arrived and carried him back.
Then suddenly, far out, a sound broke the silence
like an audience clapping in an invisible amphitheatre.
The tide had turned; little waves flipped beachward.
He ran to meet them.

EVENING AT ROSCARBERRY

1

A causeway divides the shallow lagoon.
Water slips under the four-eyed bridge
at the south end. Quiet currents change
with shifting levels.

The swans gather in a loose flock
and steer like a fleet to the causeway,
each one at the apex of the letter V,
its own watery cartouche.

They stop near the bridge; some hold
one leg out of the water
folded over on white feathers
as if resting a black oar.

They have their own language,
an urgent gurgle not a supplication,
more a pressing request with their
orange and black beaks thrust forward.

Their feathers are snow white like the skin
of children lost off these rocks
fifty years ago;
their names are set on stone slabs
near the sun-bench facing the sea;

ways of remembering in stone,
ways of remembering by swans;
lost innocents of failed aspirations;
ageless birds on grey-black water
defy the iron matrix of time.

2

Out in the lagoon, the cormorant
squats on a sandbank, black, motionless.

Three herons hold separate vantage points
and step in their sly ungainly way from
pool to pool, leave the sands close to land
for a white egret and a flock of sandpipers.

At last one heron takes flight, a glass image
against dark clouds behind Mount St Michael.

There is no gold or purple in this evening sky
yet the heron is not of our element,
water can not destroy his primal power;
like the benu bird, he wears antiquity well.

SURFACE

We live near a mountain, wreathed
shoulder high in cloud, peak twisted
above invisible villages on her side;
near an evening sea that fades to silver,
its distance merging with sky lines of
apricot, purple-blue, sloe-grey. A ship
sets out from the port for Málaga, over
undercurrents older than the Phoenicians.

Her lights unseal the darkness, unlabelled
like your skin, against my efforts to see
the elemental things making us who we are;
how we can never be other than ourselves,
burning stars, disappearing into black holes,
with only names and dates above our heads.

LOVERS

They lie where sea and sand kiss,
when the sky is faintest blue
and high and far as forever.

These afternoons she rolls between
sand and sea, her skin grows darker,
almost as dark as her hair.

She flips in and out of tiny waves
like a seal, laughing and soaking
the cool through all her pores.

Her fingers stretch to the sky
like a ballerina, light pours
down her arms like a magic wand.

Sometimes he leaves her for a while
to bring flowers from the *paseo*:
red hibiscus or pink azaleas.

All afternoon their lives merge:
she reads from her favourite book,
pours water from the cool-box.

As the sun reaches the lighthouse,
he strolls to the railing and wheels
her chair down the boardwalk.

KITESURFER

He crosses the line that divides
black and green waters roaring beachward –
ignores the rest and draws a foaming trail.

Furthest out, his single wing,
a lapis arc tipped white.

His body bends to leap the surf,
reaches to catch each thermal twist.

Other kites hang high and still,
or dive to sand in red and blue;
prince of wind and tides, the sea is his.

THE HEM OF ISLAM

Shell-white ships slip through
the Straits between Tarifa and Tangier.
Spain seems close to the African coast,
where scattered white villages fade

into Moroccan foothills, patterned
like the spine of a sleeping monster.
Lace-fringed tips of the Rif Mountains
lie at the vanishing point.

From these villages emigrants flee,
packed tightly into fragile *pateras*
fit for less than six. At night they risk
their lives against the undercurrents

of the Straits of Death. Some survive,
others are washed up on the beach.
The nameless ones, buried three deep
in a graveyard above the town.

Along Costa de la Luz, waves
roll towards creamy-silver sand,
wide coils of transparent turquoise,
like tunnels of thin glass. They seethe

up the beach and splash into fronds
of frothy snakes near the Moorish castle,
built to a God of mercy and clemency
when few Christians knew this place.

FIRE AND ICE

Light through lattice
throws a keener dazzle;
we rise to sun and snow,
sea and palms; a chill
makes marble sting
bare morning soles.

From the terrace,
the mountain edges gleam
like knives in the sky
beyond San Pedro.

The midday air still,
so clean and cold
as if a glacial spirit
had lost its way,

stranded on Torrecilla,
revelled in pinsapo forests
of the Sierra de las Nieves,
inhaling scent of trees

LAND AND LIGHT

LANDSCAPE WITH LIGHT

Fields covered by winter floods;
flat *callas* shimmer under latent power
from January sun and stretch to
the tower of Killeroran graveyard.

The water gleams like melted mercury;
billions of rounded diamonds
vibrate and throb in newfound glory
over acres of lost grass.

It is the triumph of water over earth
as it was in the beginning. The land
is a massive lake now, but like lakes
on Titan, is not what is seems.

I want to keep this day forever, this light,
this water, this cold January noon;
I know when I return again, the fields
will be greening for summer meadows,

as if nothing had happened at all,
as if nothing has happened to me.
I take my camera from my pocket
and rest on an old whitethorn,

its trunk roped with ivy arms
so the ivy is a green bush
at the top, revelling in winter's
temporary triumph.

I move my camera across the waterscape,
from Killeroran tower to the slopes
of Cloonakellig on the opposite side
of the river. Here my grandfather

grew wheat to pay the landlord's rent;
careful, tight-fisted neighbours buried
new sovereigns each autumn
under flagstones of their kitchen floors.

Even when my grandfather left the place,
sold the thatched house and farm
to come to Garrier on this side
of the river, my father and his brothers

kept a boat under the salleys
where the stone wall ended,
and rowed back each Sunday
to the village of their birth.

The row of tall salleys between
the River Field and Slough Field
is there; only the ghost of the wall
my grandfather built remains,

a scatter of white-patched stones
blotched with tufts of black moss.
The fields are different too, moulded
by the markings of the flood.

The water in the Slough Field
is shaped to a long rectangle,
where a marooned hillock
becomes a tree-filled island;

its trees are old and clawed;
their reflection in floodwater
like a light-filled lithograph –
still, stamped, holding eternal pose.

A swan floats by this fluid facsimile,
keeps close to the island's curve,
with wings and feathers puffed
like hoisted ghost-galleon sails.

When she has left my sight,
the photographs are finished.
Roped arms of the ivy press
my back as if wanting to tie

me into their twisted patterns;
to become rooted in this place
forever watching seasons pass
to music of endlessly arguing swans.

GRANDFATHER

Today, Mother told me the whole story:
how he died on Valentine's Day
the year after she married.

The doctor warned him years before
that his heart needed to mend.

But he could not change his ways –
a shepherd by trade and nature.

So when the timber pile ran low, he took
the saw from the nail behind the door

and crossed the field to the plantation,
where he worked all day in the bitter cold.

At dusk he carried armfuls of beech and ash
and stacked them near the water-barrel

at the gable end, his head bent
against the black east wind.
It was too much for him.

SHIFTINGS

The sky is a concave blue canvas
where the painter has dabbed
a twist of white in the cool air.

By the river bank, the salley bends,
broken, black and desultory.
A water-hen flicks from the sedge
and darts further up the river.

Rows of dead reeds line the grass
as far up as the hawthorn ditch.
In one pile, a black plastic oar
lies hidden. Half the blade is gone.

I carry it with me; it will stop
a gap in a hedge or prop open
a shed door. It will never feel
the rush of river but succumb

to a new element, like the carcass
of the dead newborn lamb, hidden
near furze in the Slough Field;
its wool and outer body perfect,

but eyes and rib cage empty,
picked clean by fox and crow;
hooves smooth, legs splayed
as if resting from a frolic.

INTERPLAY

April unwraps her green skirt dotted with wild violets
and primroses in the sun-trap under the bare beeches.

Trees are slow to leaf, only a line of salleys skimmed
    with green.
The houses beyond the river have edged closer since
    winter.

A backwash of reeds lies stranded near Collins's
    double-ditch,
a magic carpet woven by the flood in brown and ash.

Shallow water in the Slough glints like a sharpened
    sickle,
reflecting old trees, gnarled and twisted against
    change.

FLOOD

It rained for days in May;
the curve of the river at the rusty metal bridge
drowned the fields around Talbot's Castle.

The path to the water's edge traces a high
    embankment,
a railway without tracks fading as land grows boggy.

Below the path, whitethorns stand in green-black
    water,
branches draped with heavy blossoms, heads bowed,
as if trying to find their roots.

The path ends; water blocks the way to bridge and
    castle,
though morning light brings the old walls closer.

Each year, ivy expands the ruins to a green
    sarcophagus
on the flat landscape, smothers what it clings to, seals
    the past.

FUSION

The door to summer opens;
seas of starred grass flow
down the old railway banks.

The whitethorn branches wait
like tiered garlands on the skirts
of girls standing at a maypole,
to begin the Festival of Fire.

DREAMWOOD

This time of year
in the fretwork of skewed seasons,
I think of you;

trees are touched with green,
road edges banked with hailstones
like saltpetre.

Your canvas stretches on a frame,
the purple one you cut back
and repainted blue and green,
with long turquoise brush strokes;
the rim of purple remained
like a ripened bruise.

What if the vernal matrix cracks,
the calends fail, the seasons poison,
or the Arctic ice thaws, while you
paint in your house above the sea?

Will I find in your scheme
patinas of the dreamwood
we will visit at the end of May?

PEACOCK BUTTERFLY

That morning he exhausted himself on the windowpane,
tried to escape into the rain, but I kept him in;
hid him in the drawer of the walnut chest
where my Lady's looking-glass stands
over the narrow toilet-bureau.

He could not see this despite his four gorgeous eyes:
rubies at the top on a pale yellow patch,
lapis lazuli below, dark-ringed on cream.
In the toilet-bureau, my Lady's
things rest on deep-blue velvet:
a clothes brush from Sevenoaks,
wooden tweezers, midget teazle,
and a satin photograph-case.

In the afternoon sun I held him at the window sill.
He remained quite still; his locked wings
quivered to perfume from the garden.
His feet clung to my warm palm,
but he did not show his eyes, so
I placed him in the open drawer;
he could escape at will to roses,
fuchsia and montbretia.

By evening he was gone;
my Lady's looking-glass can't tell me where;
but the bureau's deep-blue velvet is the colour
of his lower eyes. That night I dreamt of sleeping
in a summer meadow, my body covered with butterflies.

KNOCKANARE

It took less than a week to skin the sods
from the sloping acres of O'Donnell's field.

By late summer the green had bled to reddish-brown,
the topsoil heaped in pyramids at the lowest end.

This morning's crow-call over Knockanare loosens
layers of my fading sleep, draws me back to world time.

I reach the roadside as machines rev up,
see the last fifty yards of ditch: hawthorn, ash, rosehip,

split roots jutting from flattened earth
like lengths of broken bones.

THE CHANGE

Summer hesitates – just briefly –
like the missed breath of a sleeping child.

On the row of trees behind the manse,
a blush of leaves, the size of a tablecloth, has turned
    gold.
No one cares or sees as yet; time's tireless finger
    writes on.

Each morning sun grows a jot weaker through the
    window,
the angle lower, soaking the crimson carpet
with shifting trapezoids of heat.

HUNTER'S MOON

Past the graveyard, over the fields
of Scribley Hill, the rising moon
is tangled in clumps of trees and gorse.

Cathedral bells ring low and hollow
across the town. When I reach the hilltop
the moon waits, newly born from the bay.

I inhale her full glory, bow to worship
the ancient huntress as she begins
her journey across empty, silent, fields.
I want to ask the childhood question,
'is there anybody on the moon, Daddy?'

We are walking back from the tillage field
with a cart full of barley sheaves.
His cap is tilted back, his jacket
in the crook of his arm, the collar-stud
of his white shirt loosened.
We stop at the haggard gate.

Then, as now, the moon gives no answers;
she rises little by little in a blue-grey sky,
the colour of an infant's eyes.

When I turn back, her light follows me.
The town is lit in blue, red and green;
it has its answers like painted flowers
that survive when real ones have withered.

Pylons loom across the landscape,
skeletons of monsters holding up the sky.

When I reach the graveyard again,
the moon is high behind me. Her light draws
shadows from long grass, ferns and hedges.

Now, I have two shadows:
one long and thin showing the way,
the other, much closer, a shrunken self.

When I reach the back door, the moon hangs
in the mountain ash behind the outcrop of rock.

She is trapped in the branches of that magic tree,
split in its electric limbs; she has entered
each and every flaming berry.

RACHEL IN THE GARDEN

I wait for her on the narrow path
between towering artichokes.
One has flowered,
a purple-blue, big as my fist,
a giant's signet ring to taunt
the grey clouds moving west.

She arrives.
We move along the gravel path,
pull weeds here and there, leave
the bunch of scarlet poppies.
'Once I kept this clear', she says,
'but now I cannot bear
to pluck wild poppy flowers'.

We talk about the Wars,
our connections with them:
how in West Donegal
the poppy and the shamrock
are worn together;
how her father saved
the photograph of a German soldier
she hid in a book and cannot find,
but looks for still.

Down the steps she names for me
viburnum, alchemilla mollis, astilbe.
The two-hundred-year-old redwood
at the corner of the lawn.
We look across the lake at chestnut,
willow, ash, elder.
There is a longing
for autumn's colours in her voice.

LIMES

My brother cuts logs for winter fires;
his chainsaw whines and echoes
over the frosty fields of Cluain Cath.

Fine white sawdust spurts back;
it scatters over his black jacket,
across the green rubber boots
and thick red shiny gloves.
He bends over the fallen limb,
a horizontal rib snapped off.
'It had rotted at the trunk', he says,
'all these trees will go in time'.

We see where rain had lodged
in the bole and ruined the tree;
the branches arched with age,
but the slow surfeit of damp,
like innocent arsenic, filtered
into every fissure.

Once this row of limes cloaked
the road from winter sleet.
Tinkers camped under them,
on a patch of scattered sand
left when the road was tarred.

The trees dripped cold blessings
on their tents, but faces shone
from behind burning sticks.
They faced west, towards floods
in Gleann na nÉan,
and memories of solid sunsets
beyond the demesne wall.

'God between us and eating turf',
my grandmother used to say;

there it was in her prayer: fear of starvation,
of being left to the elements, like the tinkers
sleeping under black canvas curved over
hazel rods, in the shelter of the demesne wall.

In early morning rain, their fire smoke curled
from burned-out sticks, as we walked to school.
We saw cabbage leaves and rags flung in briars,
heard babies cry, sniffed sourness in heavy air.

Their wild looks scared us: faces browned by wind,
crazy hair. The women wore bright plaid shawls,
full flannel skirts with square pockets decorated
by rows of fancy buttons; their feet in sturdy boots.
My grandmother knew them well.

Some had lost their men after fights, or from falls
off carts, or from pneumonia, the disease of the chest.
They begged, sold red paper flowers on thin wire stems,
shiny tin mugs and cans. The men bartered
galvanised buckets for turf, hay, horsehair, old metal.

All summer we envied their freedom as they sauntered
in the pathway; pitied their winter misery, when inside
the door they waited for a cup of milk or cut of butter;
rain dribbled from their shawls making silver pools
on the kitchen's cement floor.

Their voices were loud and coarse, broad vowels,
guttural. No one offered them houses then.
Their men had a trade – tinker, *tincéir* –

one who worked with tin; they were respected,
needed by country women before plastic came.

'A cup of milk for the babby and I'll say a prayer for you',
the woman said, as she pulled the lid off the long tin can;
my grandmother poured it in. We smiled at the *babby*
in her shawl, quite snug; maybe her fourth or fifth.
She looked forty, was twenty-three, might never see fifty.

If she died the drinking at the funeral would last for
    days;
men full of porter, ready to fight for any reason or none;
hardship chafing the heated blood.

ADVENT

Behind the altar, three lancet windows
reach towards the dark-brown ceiling.

Midwinter sun shafts silver beams
over half-empty Sunday seats.

The scattered flock bow to their god;
but which one: the old, the new, or both?

In purple vestments, the silver-haired priest
faces the young voices in the choir-loft:

'the core of what we are is tested;
the sins of the world are washed away'.

New voices, old bodies, history inscribed
on two marble plaques:

   'the family murdered in Malahide, 1926;
   prayers for parents of a local merchant'.

The lancet windows shimmer to silver solder
round three centred quatrefoils:

six ears of wheat on lapis lazuli;
four brown sycamore leaves on crimson;
a silver chalice and host on vine leaves.

At Consecration, the after-image on my retina
dissolves into golden bars,

then pulsates into one scarlet flame
behind my closed eyes.

SILENCE WITH WORDS

The Silence

He grew up by the sea.
There were fishing boats and forests.
All day the mills whined,
sawing trees for the town down the river.

He feared the next pogrom:
his family herded into the synagogue,
door nailed up,
thatched roof set ablaze,
screams carrying north into the cool Nordic air,
to fjords he visited one lovely summer as a child.

He wished they had stayed in the long narrow channels
of deep blue water.

At last, he gathered their belongings,
stacked them on one small cart,
took a train from the town and sailed
to the hubbub of an English city.

I lost you in the city,
then could not remember
where you lived, that street
of tall, red-berried trees.
At the corner stood a child;
she took my hand, led me
to her family in the ghetto.
They made wedding dresses
that hung along a dim room;
needles and threads flecked
the blackened floorboards.
Patterns half-folded on a table
like old Chinese maps
of coasts, houses and temples.
We spread them on the floor –
I tried to think of your number,
I could only remember *nine*,
and that was not your number.
My canvas bag fell to the floor;
the red journal, I always carry,
flung open.

SAFFRON

1

Hundreds of Buddhist monks were beaten in Rangoon.
Soldiers used canes and rifle butts;
blood soaked the saffron robes
of young men with shaven heads.

2

You wave to me across the square
from beside the Campanile.
'Wait for me in the queue',
your message says.
I wait in the cold, despite the best
of late September sun.
We wrap scarves over our heads
like monks warding off blows.
The Angelus bell rings; we enter.

3

The hall is warm and noisy,
I hand in my papers under the portrait
of Elizabeth I.
'I wanted to destroy you peasants', she said,
'but thought better of it'.
'Thanks', I said, 'I am glad you didn't
and your hair looks wonderful'.
She smiled.

4

Hundreds of Buddhist monks were jailed in Rangoon.
The streets are cleared after another day of rioting.

EXIT LEFT

Over lunch we come to terms with the laws
of perpetual return, not in a cerebral sense,
but through channels of immutable intuition,
the chemistry of protean imagination.
Leavened and split between parallel lives,
we float to an inner space, your inscape
in my amniotic fluid. Connected by words
you begin the rituals of self-revelation.

Hours converge into a fabulous freeze-frame
in this other dimension we call intimacy –
for want of a better word – what other names
can we use? None have formed as yet,
only approximations in the darkness of eyes,
echoed by black olives on the blood-red dish.

SARA BARAS

An empty stage at the port side
of the ochre bullring floor;
a chattering audience in rows
of white cloth-covered chairs.

A pair of crying seagulls
cross the late night sky
towards the clear half-moon.
Then, dark-blue spotlights
fade the crowd to silence.

A vision in soft amber light;
her fabulous frame wrapped
in a long silver dress,
a looped twist of silk held
to one side of her waist.

The music of two guitars
and violins fills the bullring.
The dance begins; arms held high,
to strains of Moorish love songs,
she embraces sky and earth.

A thousand faces watch;
she unfolds *duende's* mystery;
taut sinews thrill and quiver,
her body a convergeance
of all the lines of beauty.

She loosens the silk at her waist
to become a wide swirl of skirt,
a pulsing wave of silver;
from fingertips to stamping feet,
the dancer has become the dance.

Museo Picasso Málaga

Everything in white and black except
the paintings of deconstructed bodies
reassembled in geometric overlaps;
no tenderness between objects
and humans or in the reclining nudes.
It is late afternoon when we leave
the white rooms with their spotlights
blended to the point of natural light.

The air is cool outside. Poinsettias,
stacked in high circular stands, warm
the eye. A young couple lounge
in wicker chairs outside a café, smile
at two black kittens playing on the steps
of San Agustín. They gaze into each
other's eyes, unaware of churchgoers
making their way for evening prayer.

Near the cathedral, orange trees
are bright with fruit; Christmas lights,
laced through the branches, flicker,
and oranges momentarily come alive.
Black seats under the trees are empty;
no tired tourists; no flower-sellers
seeking cents from the purse
while taking euros from the wallet.

In El Jardin, the aroma of coffee
floats around six iron pillars from a canopy
festooned with tendrils of gold stuccowork.
Pale plaster-casts of poets and writers
look down from walls above the tables;
names I do not know: *Rubio Arguilles,*
Ángel Caffarena, Salvador Rueda.

PREDATOR

Fifteen faces,
each one painted on white canvas;
faces without skin
in blue, white, red, green.

White lines intersect
below the nose of his portrait,
lines of light from crazed eyes.
Nothing can show us

the genius of this man;
how he came to be;
why women loved
and cared for him;

what women he plundered
to remake himself,
or how his work changed
as his lovers changed.

His sky, his old city,
were the things he wanted
in the end and he dreamed
of pigeons in the square

where he played,
and his father's studio
where he lined the page
to conquer nothingness.

He despised his life;
his children hated
the sound of his voice
in the empty cluttered studio.

DALÍ'S *PERSEO* – MARBELLA

Perseo brandishes Medusa's snake-ridden head,
unaware they have infested his own hair.

He stands secure in the power of strong arms,
muscular chest and thighs; the forward thrust
of his sword overshadowing his tiny genitals.

The headless Medusa lies at his feet,
fine-limbed, slender, slight-breasted,
the envy of Athena, victim of her rage.

ESCRIBIR

Around the garden of Museo Picasso
a laurel hedge blocks the laughter
of evening strollers by the Teatro Romano.

Above our heads the feathery branches
of jacarandas hide the sky; four spotlights
fixed to their trunks shine on a lectern.

The poet's words are low, gentle, liquid.
I close my eyes, feel her dreams, rivers
and memories flow round me in the dusk.

Between poems, the evening song of birds
and the pealing of bells from San Agustín,
marked time.

I open my eyes and leave her world.
A dove flies through the spotlight beam,
a ghost of grace beyond language itself.

We walk back by the Alcazaba,
I whisper, *los sueños, las memorias,*
las riberas, escribir, escribir, escribir …

EQUALITY EMERGING
a sculpture by John Behan

Arms and shoulders ready to run,
her hair and breasts loose,
she is flung free of the stone slab;
only her feet are bound.

Someone has placed daffodils
at her feet; their sap will help
clear what was never written
in stone.

The cathedral casts its shadow
towards her; it can not touch.

Behind her, Corrib waters roar
over the Salmon Weir; churned
white lips fold over the thrust of it
down to the open sea.

The Artist's House

Winter falls out of favour;
spring forces growth
against blasts of twisting hail.
Snowdrops lace the avenue,
Minerva's statue sways
near the latticed summerhouse.

Rows of Japanese prints
of Mt Fuji lead to the kitchen.
Tory Island paintings hang
over the dresser; aerial views,
plain as the Picasso plate –
work of a man who wanted
to draw like a child.

Afternoon light grazes across
the dining room's red carpet,
under *Dark Evening* by Boudet.
The paintings of Zoran Music
still hold shadows of that time,
when the slaughter at Dachau
shut the eyes of innocence,
when hands were blackened
by invisible lives.

TWO POLISH PAINTINGS

In *Strange Garden*,
a mother and servant stand
in the shade of apple trees,
to watch a small boy at play.
Flower garlands loop
through lower branches;
an enormous dragonfly
overhangs mother and child.
The boy is bathed in light.
He ventures forward
as if to leave the painting,
but there is no sky, no way out.
He is trapped in Eden.

The hapless *Partridges*,
all eighteen of them,
move into the snowscape.
Leaderless and lost,
their dark brown feathers
no match for Siberian winds.
The snow is not white,
more a bleached sepia.
Perhaps some farmer's boy
will spot them in time.

CHRISTENING DAY
for Grace

That first Sunday in October,
fog cloaked the drumlin country,
dense, dark, cold as winter.

For a while, the lake below the road
merged with the fog in a new dimension,
a kind of *unus mundus*.

I waited until light seeped through
and then I saw it –
a dark prow gliding from the left bank.

I began to think of Lake Galilee,
of a figure walking on water,
of shoals of fish and breaking nets.

Then the boat vanished as strangely
as it had come, so did the fog;
I could see cattle on the hill the other side.

A single swan took flight across the water,
just above the surface, hypnotised by it,
unable to find the lift of air.

All these sights and more will be yours one day,
this is only your Christening Day.

TIME OF WATER

Think only of white, snow and ice;
its weird transparent grip on skin
as if magnetised for a moment, clings
its cold lust for warm blood, the need
to enter and dissolve elsewhere;
and when the lake froze two years ago,
a young Polish lad slid out across the ice
dragged by two Alsatians on silver chains.

Children in houses near the lake
stood with faces close to window panes,
their mouths like tiny circles, transfixed
by fear in their bellies that the centre-ice
would creak, crack and suck them down
to where torpid glass-eyed pike eased by.

LEAVINGS

These will be left after me:

a book of poems,
someone will remember
or read, then cast aside;

my name,
wiped by weather,
unlike the lost Catalan language
of the Andalucian Jews,
found nine hundred years later;

well buried bones,
forever earthed in a family plot,
not like the lovers in a shallow grave
outside the abbey walls,
her severed head on his chest,
her womb with child.

Nothing left
of the deadly pearls – fear and hate –
buried in heart, gut and bowel;
unless, like bubbles of quicksilver,

they have already escaped,
and scattered across the table
one evening after dinner.

SNOWGRAVE

Fresh footprints in old snow
there for two weeks, topped
with crystals from Siberian air.

Headstone crosses gleam
under the striped sky dome;
grey, cream and peach clouds
smother the shrivelled sun.

This winter, your first gone;
your long bones stretched
under a frozen blanket;
plants withered at your feet.

You are beside him now after
thirty years, not touching;
the clay wall between you,
down there away from us,

far from the cosy bed,
and blankets you loved for years
to pull up around your head,
'for a little snooze', you'd say.

All those mornings I watched you enjoy,
knowing you would go,
soon.
Even then,
I was mourning you too long.

BEGINNINGS

I

Waiting

A sudden seasickness in the belly;
a clarity, an energy to put in place
what was tossed, disordered, ended;
to set the Christmas tree to right
with multicoloured lights running
through branches, winking behind
spinning baubles of red, green, gold.
Without knowing why, I wait.

Silent evening's freezing air swallows
the bleak hills and faint blue-pink of sky,
prepares for dark and midnight's black ice.
You wait for the warm rush of water,
a channel unplugged, an early spasm
to start you on your firstborn's journey.

II

Signs

A swarm of crows in early morning
jabbering, falling, drifting, rising;

banks of daub by the river's edge
glow from grey to sterling silver;

flames dance in the open fire
as midday sunlight is lanced by rain;

cherries gleam in new-made bread,
my christening fruit in a time of snow;

copper coins on a red music case,
with a ray of sun spin to gold;

cerise blossoms on a silken scroll
with characters in elegant Mandarin:

 the world is perfect, as the blossom is perfect,
 perfect and generous and good.

III

Birth

Low grey morning floods recede
from the fields beyond the river;
streams draws back from the plain
to the seas insatiable desire to birth,
to break water; you begin your first
voyage down the birth canal to light:
small head pressed by pelvic bones,
body slippery with amniotic fluid;

waves of muscle-spasm push you,
the waters warm around you,
body glazed in blood and vernix
as you meet steel morning light;
the purple cord pulses with old life
ready to be severed, to set you free.

IV

Light of the Sun

From dark of womb to brilliant light,
cry of birth to a winter's world,
grasp of fingers unknown to touch,
touch on skin as yet untouched;

delicate lips of an angel's mouth,
scent of freshness new as spring,
new generation begin your song,
balm to souls beyond the grave;

I wish you:
breath of life,
care of heart,
strength of hand,
song of songs,
beauty of mind,
knowledge gleaned,
wisdom's joy,
nature's love.

V

Christmas Present

For months you moved and kicked,
invisible, throbbing, stretching,
flexing in your airless cavern
like a space voyager;
your tiny hand-wave on the scan,
a prenatal semaphore –
your first message to the world
from under your Mother's heart.

Lulled by love's great vibrations,
all those dark safe days, were you
feeling, thinking, hearing the sounds
of the outer world, were you happy
or afraid?

Today, your smooth cheeks
have sunlight on them; you cry
as your kicking feet sense the change
from warm to cold, your arms flail

as you grasp the swollen breast,
not knowing the joy and pain
of this release that follows a line
old as Asherah, the tree of life.

VI

Homecoming

All morning, ice melts from footpaths
as winter breezes probe suburban gardens,
bend miniature trees, toss their tiny apples.

The low sun thaws frost-glazed roofs,
shaping similar geometric patterns:
chevrons, lozenges, triangles, squares.

I wait for your baby cry, to stroke your head
and hands, to feel the joy of your sleeping self,
the pointless thrust of your mouth to my chest.

Then you are there when I open the door,
as if you had always been, asleep in your
new red pram in a newly discovered world.

VII

Metsu to Mothercare

This winter I am not in the gallery
with the Metsu paintings, puzzling
over the amorous message in
A Woman Reading a Letter;

or finding the wry symbolism
in *The Hunter's Gift.* I remember
The Vegetable Market in Amsterdam,
as I face the Grafton Street crowds
on my way to Mothercare.

A young Chinese man helps me find
tiny vests, cellular blankets, muslin towels.

I buy your first rattle.

ACKNOWLEDGEMENTS

Acknowledgements are due to the editors of the following publications in which a number of these poems, or versions of them, first appeared:
Poetry Ireland Review, The SHOp, Cyphers, Revival, The Scríobh Anthology, Sixteen after Ten Anthology, The Forward Book of Poetry 2011.

My sincere thanks to the following for their help and support: Errigal Writers, Monica Strina, Jackie Blackman, Mary Melvin Geoghegan, Marcella Molloy, Michael and Mary Silke, Rathmines Writers and The Francis Ledwidge Society.

A very special thanks to my husband Jim and family for their love and patience.

Mary Turley-McGrath grew up in Mount Talbot on the Galway/Roscommon border and now lives in Letterkenny, Co. Donegal. She was a teacher with Donegal Vocational Education Committee and was awarded a Masters Degree in Education Management from the University of Ulster.

Her first collection of poetry, *New Grass under Snow,* was published by Summer Palace Press in 2003. Mary was awarded an M.Phil in Creative Writing from Trinity College Dublin in 2009. Her work has appeared in journals and anthologies including *The Forward Book of Poetry 2011.* Mary's poems have been successful in national and international competitions and have been broadcast on RTÉ Radio 1. She was the first recipient of the Annie Deeny Award through The Arts Council/An Chomhairle Ealaíon and The Arts Council of Northern Ireland. She completed three residencies in the Tyrone Guthrie Centre, Annaghmakerrig. Her reading venues include the Irish Writers' Centre, the Old Library of Trinity College Dublin and the Art Bar, Toronto.

Forget the Lake is her second collection of poetry.